TWO FACED; A VILLAIN, A HERO.

NIHARA SREE ANEESH

Made with ♥ on the Notion Press Platform
www.notionpress.com

Dedicated to those who need it.

Contents

Preface

This is going to be the most simplest, basic book on how to find yourself better when it comes to people (and yourself).

Despite being a 7th grader and not much on with the experience of life, I've Observed quite enough, saw and learned how a few things worked and decided to write this.

That wouldn't also just be the reason as well. As someone who suffered from depression for more than a year, I needed to escape from it, So writing is where I decided to make my stop for now.

although there is a stop for each; It's just a basic plain book, I'd recommend this to someone who's still in school especially.

(One thing to make sure, That In this book all the information won't be present much; But I've stated everything I possibly could think of.)

Besides of my story, Why is the title so...

You are the One choosing your Way of life, and You have Every power of it.

Other people will be reading this too, Which is that you and them are different. You have control of your life, Don't control other lives. "Two Faced- A Villain, A hero." Explains That At least every person we see Has been Bad in someone Else's Life Before; you have too. Every Innocent person you see, Can lie Secrets which Doesn't seem Like something that they would do.

Two Faced, All of us Are two Faced.

As you wake up everyday, you are going to see people; it's either the people you see everyday or people you may not know. If you are going to talk to these people, you might be judging them...Or maybe not since you might talk to that Person everyday.

And as us Humans, we have different opinions on different people, and different types of people you meet, might have different opinions about you.

Let's say you have helped a person financially, how would they be? In most expectations, they'd appear more friendly, Maybe start to talk to you more and might try their best to repay you back. And moving forward to another story; Let's also say that you have made many empty promises to somebody...How would they be? They'd most likely want to avoid you, Talk behind your back and Stay strong that you are a bad person.

See how both people have different opinions about you?

The first person we've talked about would've seen you as a hero, someone who you helped when they were at their lowest. On the other hand, the other person sees you as a villain, someone...evil.

-That's life. You can't be perfect.

We Show different types of energy to other people, Some Nice, Some not; Which we Seem like A Hero, genuine, filled with Personality and Character. But to the others, We are A Villain, Someone they Might Have misunderstood, Or by something you've Done in the past which they'd still remember.

You usually do this because you've automatically kept "Roles and Behaviour" For Every Person you've met.

It's Like talking to someone New, It depends on how you
feel...At the moment, How would you Like to react
to that Person; Happy? Angry? Your choice.

None of us Know What Can happen.

CHAPTER ONE

People are memories.

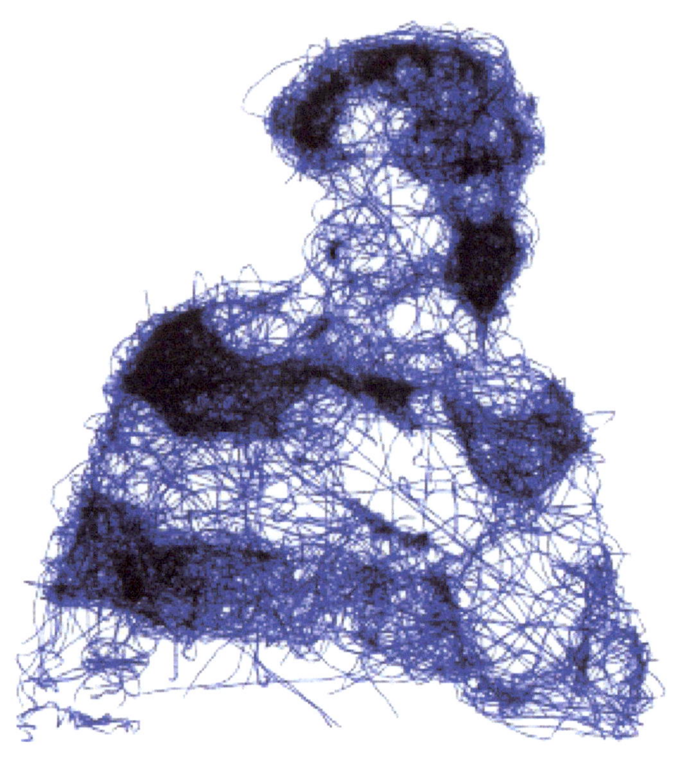

When new people enter our life, New memories and Options will surround us. What thing to look around is How Does the Person Talk/Speak With Other people? Who are the People She/he Talks to? What Qualities Does the Person have?

Despite we humans tend to judge first on what we see or are meant to believe, trying to get to know the person will result better.

People Come With Different Mindsets, And Some Of them

Might Not Be Looking For anyone to talk to at first, **thats what makes us special.**

“ Never Judge A Book by its Cover. “

Now we’ve All Heard that Quote, It’s everywhere. But Most of us Do it Unknowingly. So, First Impressions Come Really Handy here.

Be yourself. Talk calmly, Doesn’t have to result in anything big.

This is When The person Might come to you with An Friendly Approach, Therefore The Person Here Is most Likely to Be calm around you, Knowing that Now the Person Might show their True colors or..Just Be the Same!

If They Start To seem Odd, Doesn’t Talk to you Anymore, Then Never, no, NEVER Go after them. You shouldn’t destroy your personality for anyone.

But Make sure, If they do something wrong, Some Behaviour That you Just don’t like, Don’t go After them. Would you rather lose your personality or lose someone? exactly.

One thing to cover here mostly is

Toxic People, Are everywhere, Literally, It’s Not even Hard To spot one, It’s the Same too, You get used, And then Try to heal The next Few months, They leave you,They Point at you, Throw Dirt on your Name, But I’m Here to Just Tell A few About them If you think you’re also Doing something wrong which was Mentioned Here, It’s Never, NEVER too late to Become A Better Person

(I’ve Kept My own Names for them, And I’m Talking about all The toxic People I’ve met in my life here so..yeah.)

The one thing I’ve understood about rude or toxic people is that, **they weren’t always like this, Its trauma that kills us and causes us to change.** Some people are hurt so bad in the past that the past had eaten them whole and make them think that they are supposed to this the same and do it to others. Which Is why I mostly stay calm, Cause by looking at them, you wouldn't just know what they went through.

1 - The Gossip

At least Every one Of us has Talked Bad About someone. It could be Someone Who Doesn't like you so you Talk about them, Or You talk Bad about them, Which gives them A trigger to Talk about you, Badly.

This Person Has A Intention Of Talking Bad About People, Everyone Does Actually, But This Person Has Much More Of An Negative Mind, And Might Talk Total Nonsense About people.

Keep in Mind that People Who Give Off This Vibe Usually Won't Have People Around Them Since The Person Listening to this Might Just Back-Stabs The person And talks Bad about them, Perhaps. And You Lashed it Off to Them, So, It's A Process From One Person To another..

The Best Thing you Can Do When you Want to Talk about How Bad Someone Is, Is to Use the Method " Praise publicly, Criticize privately. "

Talk to Someone who you trust about it, But not Someone Who's Good friends with the "New Kid" , Then you Might Get yourself Into Something.

2 - The "They And I Are My priority."

These Type Of People Are ones Which Cares About Themselves, And only There group of friends, I mean we all Do, But This One Takes it too far.

Imagine, You and Someone Were Talking about what you did On the Weekends, You Said you Went on the Beach And they Said They Went With their Group to the Mall, And then, This Self n' Them Absorbed Person From the Group Come tagging Along And Starts Somewhat "Flexing" It to you,

" We went on That ride..uh..It's some kind of Ride which you always Wanted to go to."

" Omg Me And The Girls Went To a Stationary Shop And Got Matching Pouches! "

" Oh Trust me, We we're About to Call you, But I knew you would Say No. "

and then You'd Of course Have the Empty feeling in your Heart, But NEVER Let that Get to you. Nothing Ever Lasts Forever, And That Thing Wouldn't Stay for Long.

NOTE : REMEMBER That If you've gone out with your friends, Always Keep It Simple If you are going to talk about it, Because People Aren't really interested about it, Or they would've been hurt if you didn't call them, etc.

3 - "I'm Never Satisfied"

Say That You Won Some Huge Competition And Every Single Friend Of yours Claps And Cheers For You, But At The Distance Of The Crowd Cheering On You, You See A Friend of yours, Not Very Close To You, Staring, But Not In A Good way.

You Quickly Realize that They are Jealous, Or Not satisfied, Oh, Cause they didn't like you winning? Is it something else? You decide to Go and talk to them.

"Oh, it's nothing, I'm thinking of something else." "Oh you Won? Ok. Congrats."

(KNOW THAT THIS IS NOT ACCURATE CAUSE THERE MIGHT BE SOMETHING ELSE PERSONAL GOING ON WITH THEM.)

But If You're Sure It's Jealousy, Then You'll Have to Avoid This person.

This Person Might Take Everything Seriously, Maybe Might not Even take Themselves As "Happy". You should Know That Even The Small Wins That You accomplish, Like Winning A Competition at school, Or Maybe Finishing A Huge Project, You should Be Smiling, Cause If you Never Smile At Those Small Wins, Never Expect yourself big.

If you are Happy for Someone Else's Success, There's Also A Huge Chance of You Stay Truly Happy and Being Successful At something!

"Happiness cannot be traveled to, owned, earned, worn or consumed. Happiness is the spiritual experience of living every minute with love, grace, and gratitude - Denis Waitley."

3 - The Manipulator

They usually Just Leave you, But make you Feel Guilty, Used and leave you, Right there. They Don't Appreciate What You Do, They Suck Energy And Time Out of you. They'll be Hard to Spot Since They Treat You As A friend. They'll Know What you Like, What you do, Who you talk to, But They Use This For Their Advantage.

These People, At the Same time, Won't be Hard to find and trust me, There guys Can Break you, Real bad.

" The clothes You wear Looks Poor "

Insecurity.

Insecurity Is A Normal Part in Most Lives, And Society is What Makes It More...Concerning? The Only Thing I wanna Say for This One Is, Don't go Breaking People's Hearts.

If They Apologize But don't Change, It's pure Manipulation.

4 - Breadcrumbing

Had A Friend Promise you Stuff like "We'll Stay like This forever" or "I promise That I Wouldn't Hurt you"

Now These Can be True, But what If they Break it?

The Term "Breadcrumbing" Means That At The Start, They Come To You Engaged, Happy But They Disappoint and Leave you with Empty Promises.

These People Most Likely Don't Understand The Meaning of "Trust" or "friendship". And they Go after One Person, Then another, Then another, It goes Around.

So, When you're Making a promise, Think Before You understand What All could happen If you couldn't do it, Making it Sure that You're Also Able to Do it in time, Or whatever The Situation goes.

NOTE : If Someone Was Not There In Your Lows, Then Never Include Them In Your Success, NEVER.

"No one is born ugly, we just live in a judgemental society" -

5 - The One That can Never Stop Lying

- " Honesty, Sometimes, Is NOT the Best Policy ". -

Yes, SOMETIMES, It's Not the Best Policy.

But Lying Includes Its Disadvantages too.

Even The Most Simplest Questions "Oh, you don't know That Trend?" Can be Just said "yes" Even if they don't know About it

Yes, Nowadays They Lie, Just to Fit in.

I Can't Blame Them, Cause They'd Just Want to Fit into Society The Way they want to. People Think That If you don't Know A Trend, People Wouldn't Think You're Cool..?

Whatever It is, It's Always Nice to Follow trends to Keep up, But Know that Being yourself, Comes A Long Way Of Being Awesome. Of Course.

CHAPTER TWO

PERSONAILTY.

Everyone Has Their Way of Shining, Whether It Comes To Their Smile, How They Speak, The Way They Treat People, Just Humans, Take That Thing A Bit More in Detail.

- Never. Show. off.

This Is One Of the Biggest Red Flags You Could See in A person. This is A serious no.

There are 2 Meanings for this;

You Show off, And People Get it, Or You show off, But you don't mean it,

Besides, If someone Does Show Off, You Might Have A Feeling that you'd Want it too. Just Think about all the things She/he Has never had and you did, Something..Positive!

- Socialize.

If you ask me, this Is A pretty Hard thing to do. I do Have Social Anxiety, And it Isn't Cool. My Heart goes pretty fast when I see A lot of people I don't know, But this all (kinda) stops When I'm with the friends I know.

The Main Thing About "Standing out" is When People Are the Huge Part in This Mission. Oh and, It doesn't Just Have To Be All The Popular Kids You Should Be Talking To, Talk To Someone Pretty Quiet, Or Someone Who Isn't

Popular, Remember Popular Isn't Just The Only Main Thing There, But To Be Kind To Everyone You see. Maybe Even the people Who've done you bad, it's simply called maturing.

- Breadcrumbing

Had A Friend Promise you Stuff like "We'll Stay like This forever" or "I promise That I Wouldn't Hurt you"

Now These Can be True, But what If they Break it?

The Term "Breadcrumbing" Means That At The Start, They Come To You Engaged, Happy But They Disappoint and Leave you with Empty Promises.

These People Most Likely Don't Understand The Meaning of "Trust" or "friendship". And they Go after One Person, Then another, Then another, It goes Around.

So, When you're Making a promise, Think Before You understand What All could happen If you couldn't do it, Making it Sure that You're Also Able to Do it in time, Or whatever The Situation goes.

NOTE : If Someone Was Not There In Your Lows, Then Never Include Them In Your Success, NEVER.

"No one is born ugly, we just live in a judgemental society" -

- Personality; On spot.

Personality Is What Makes The Person, A Person. Personality Isn't all About kindness, What you like, What you do at home, Your Favorite Color, All these Make A Human.

Some Ways You Should Avoid Having "this" As Your Personality.

Rude

Most Of us don't Seem To accept this, But some of them look at the person, Thinking As if It's 'Cool' Or something.

Being Rude Can Capture The Attention of Many, But it just..Isn't right.

Maybe Hatred is something you'll be Going through If you're going to stay like that.

Some People Might Think you're Cool for Being Rude, But Slowly, They'll understand that You're not A good person.

"Holding on to anger is Like Grasping A Hot Coal with the Intent of Throwing it At Someone Else; you are the one Getting burned."

Gautama Buddha (563-483 BC)

- Founder of Buddhism.

- The Wanna-Be Mature

I've seen This In A Friend Once, And this One always Has Something to Say, Technically Thinks About Keeping herself On top And Think She/He Has to Look Down On others, Thinking Other people are "Immature"

But This Person Keeps The People close to her, When she/he thinks that Person Is "Mature".

She/he But has Great Confidence, (even Over Confidence if you want to mention it like that-)

The Thing About Life Is not to Be Serious, Sometimes You'll Need To Be, But You'll Have and Need To Find Yourself Happy. No matter what, You'll Feel Happy or Sad at times, Life Gives the Chance To Express, Expose and Understand All Feelings when it comes to humans.

- Stand Tall.

It's not Like Everything Is going to Fall into Place Exactly How you wanted it to be. Nobody Close, Or Not In Any Friend Groups? Well So what?! You Can Be Someone That You Want To Be, Without Anyone's Hand To Reach out.

You Should Know That Standing Alone, And Staying Bold Is Really Awesome if you think about it, So what If You Couldn't Find Someone? Look for Someone Else! And what if you don't..Just Be yourself! All The Wonders You could do By yourself, Where Your Mind, And Only Your Mind Can Choose without Anyone Controlling you, You are free to be Yourself, physically, Mentally.

Oh and, Before You Go Judging Someone Else, We All are Bad In Someone's Story. You could Name Somebody Who's Done you wrong, Or you've done them wrong.

Everyone Has Made A Mistake, And You've definitely Done One too. I'm Saying this again, That we all Are made And brought Here to Express Feelings, And To know How Every one of them feels like, Anger, Sadness, Joy, Everything.

- Sometimes, Silence Is the Best Response.

Imagine A Fight Between Someone and Someone else Which you don't Have Much Clue About, It's most Likely That you Stand and watch, but some of us Tend to put Ourselves in a circle for attention. Now In this case, Don't go Too far. Cause It's Quite uh..Embarrassing.

- Speak out Your Opinions

When you Speak And Tell your Opinions, And they Sound pretty Cool, Then People Are going to have A Say a lot about you (in a Good way Of Course)

If you're going to just Stay Quiet, People Aren't going to Approach You as much as you think they'd do. Sometimes, Getting out of that Comfort Zone Is going to help.

- Take Feedback; Not All Of It.

We Humans Come with Different Mindsets, And Different Mindsets, Different Opinions and Think-wise.

Some Of Our People (Friends, Close friends), Might Have Things to say In Which Can make A Better Person, Something you might not see, But they do.

But Do Understand Who you're Listening to, If it's Something you think That You don't need to change, Then Don't!, Your Mind, Your heart and your body, It's all Yours.

- Don't Leave the Old Ones Behind.

This Is One Of The Most Back-stabbed Behaviors You Could do.

If you've Made new Friends, Stayed Close Enough, Never, NEVER, Leave the Old Friends Behind (If They did mean Something..really Amazing to you back then.)

The Thing is, Though new friends, Pretty Settled, But you never Know When They Stop Opening Their Hand To yours.

And Imagine If your "New friends" Left you behind, Who else Is there you could Go to? Parents, Siblings, Of course, But the Friend Status Goes down, Rapidly.

So, Never Forget about your Past, When It Comes To Those Who Gave You A Whole New Feeling, Those Things That Made You Happy, The Times you fell, And those Memories.

- Most Friendships That Are Built By Gossip, Does not work.

Gossip Is when you talk about A person, Whether good, Bad, or whatever. And friendships That are Made like this Usually Ends Up back to Strangers.

If the Friendship Only Relies On Gossip, Don't Scream Out Everything out on this Person/Group. Main Chances Are that they Will Come back-stab By and Most Likely Just Leave you there, Making you look Like A Bad person.

" People Will Forget what you said, People will forget what you did,But people Will Never Forget how you made them feel."

Maya Angelou

= Memoriest, Poet and civil rights activist.

CHAPTER THREE

IGNORANCE.

Sometimes, People don't deserve to see us smile, or be a part of our lives.

Or sometimes, People ignore us.

Ignore/Ignoring Is A Simple Term Work That you/ Someone Decides or forces themselves to Not Take Notice of.

You Could Be Ignoring A Friend Of You Which You Had A fight/Argument With Last week, Not Maybe Just Not Trying to Meet Eyes with Someone which you don't Know At a Store.

To Check if Someone Is Ignoring You, It's Quite Simple, Talk to Them And if you see slight Changes, Like No Interaction with the eyes, Voice Goes a Bit into the "serious" and Cut-Shorts The Conversation.

When This Does Happen, Understand That you should not be Talking to the person much.

NOTE : Sometimes, they maybe Might not be talking to you because Maybe there's Something you did wrong. Or on the other hand, Something might be going on Between Them.

So, Don't Just Assume It.

1 - If you're Wrong, Accept it.

If Someone is Ignoring You, It's Most Cause That You've Done Something Wrong (in Most Cases.) You've done Something Wrong, Then you Should go out and Apologize. But If You Are Thinking Maybe It ain't cool To Apologize At the moment, Then It's..Okay..I guess?

Behind All of this, One thing To Make sure is that During the Silence Between you and them, If you are the one Supposed to Apologize, Then Never Try To Trouble Them. Try Staying Silent, Don't tell other people to ignore the Person or Talk bad behind them, Just.Stay.Silent.

2 - Don't Respond Right away

Ignoring Comes In all forms, But if you still talk to them (Half Ignoring-half not) Then it's Most likely That You'll see their text, but not Respond Right away. This Gives Them Some Kind Of understanding.

3 - Just, Don't care.

Maybe, If it's Someone you Really loved and trusted, Ignoring is Tough. And will Damage you Mentally, But, If you Show that you care, You'll be seen As A puppy following its owner.

" Be careful because when you buy shoes for someone, They Might just Kick Dirt at you with the Same shoes you bought them. "

(Name not Found)

4 - Get Engaged with Something else.

If Ignoring is hard for you, Try out something new.

Try something which forgets about that person/ somebody, Try To Maybe Get over with it And Make Friends With other people.

5 - Facial Expressions and Body language.

Even In the olden days, This is the most Oldest Trick To make someone Know that They're Ignoring you.

If you Do Know that Person Is someone around, Just Look at something or Talk with someone else, They might just Think That You're doing better than them (this Might sound good If you're one of them Who Seeks Revenge)

If you Accidentally Make Eye Contact, And they do too; Then Try Giving The "Stare". Lock your eyes so you Look Intimidating.

Don't smile When your Around them.

Smile Around the People you care about, Cause If you Receive love, you'll have to give it back, That's how Friendships work.

If you do Talk to them, Don't keep The Conversation up. If they Keep asking questions (Starting a Conversation) keep Short and simple answers to their questions, Or just..Don't talk to them at all, Oh and , While talking to Them, Keep yours arms Crossed, Death Look, Emotionless, and look as if the Person Is boring.

This Can Hurt them Mentally, So Before doing any of this, Know that you're Correct in this situation, Or else You'll suffer later.

Though we won't and can't be perfect; We Can try keeping it A good level.

Make them know that you're Changing. ; Of course, Carry your Old Interests with you, But try something else new, Will Totally give them a feel of Emptiness Once you get good at it.

Don't Use people; Don't talk about it to your Friends That you Use one Person for Love, another one for Money, or Anything really else. If you do, You'll lose the Friends you have now, And the people you've "Used"

Friends are people Who change you; Let's Say A friend of yours is Really Manipulative, And slowly as you get closer to them, The sooner You'll be A clone of them, = On the other hand, If you make friends With A good person,

You'll become one of them too. Society Changes you, so, Choose wisely.

Be there When people Need you; Cause One day, Yourself, Might Just be in A Bad place, But with No one Able to reach a Hand out to you, And it's not just able, No one Would want to..

Apologize when you're wrong, Otherwise, Don't. ; Apologizing for something you did wrong and Making it Happen Is A Huge Effect on How the other person Sees You, If you don't apologize, It's most likely They're going to just Have Negative sight on you.

Be Forgiving, But don't misuse it. ; Yes, Forgiving is An Amazing thing, Asking the person/somebody To Start over and Live better and Do good In that Relationship. But if you do Forgive too much, Every single threat That Might be Gone for A while WILL come Back at you. Every.Single.Thing.

Sometimes, Karma will do their Job. ; If you Do Believe In Karma, Then This Might be Helpful. Sometimes, There is No use of you shouting And Banging your Head for them, Karma, Can Literally Do their Job.

Anger Isn't Everything. ; Just like The one on Top, Karma Is Just the Answer here, Sometimes Anger is The Answer, But Silence is The Answer to any smart Situation.

CHAPTER FOUR

Maintenance in Friendship.

If you are A friend to someone, Then Understanding Them, making them Feel welcomed into your life, Comes a Long way into Maintaining a Relationship.

Just Like Maintenance For an Damaged house, A gate for A Mansion, Maintenance In friendships is also A thing. "Maintenance" is When you and That person Should Come together, Building it strong. And if both or One of them doesn't maintain It, then Things can't go up after that.

Maintaining it is Quite simple, Talk to each other everyday, Talk about things in common, Understand Each Other, Make them feel worthy Brings A Strong Bond between them. But if nothing of that Happens,

Then you can find yourself and that Person, Slowly drifting away from the friendship. It's Like the Heart And Brain Of A Human, Without the Brain, Life Would Be Impossible To Get Through Daily, And The Heart, Without it, The Term "Life" Wouldn't be A thing.

1 - Flatter them

Whenever you find something cool about them, Simply, Compliment. Whether it's how they look today, Their Hair, Or Really..Anything!

It Makes Them Feel More Happy Around You, A friend who finds everything amazing about you, should make them definitely Tag along with you.

2 - Communication.

Talk, talk ,talk. Talking is the only thing That Brings it together. Communication Brings People, Cultures Together; Imagine a world without talking...damn.

3 - Accept that Even Much Effort might go to waste.

Though you might want that Friendship to last, The other Person Also Has to agree whether They'd want to stay and Keep going, Or Break it apart.

4 - Be A Good listener and Speaker.

Just Like Communication, Try letting them talk about what they want, And let you get the Same advantage From them. If you do not let A person Speak, Or a Person does not Let you speak; you or Them are most likely to drift apart.

But apart from this, Sometimes, They will feel like letting go, of you. One is Thing is to NEVER Force them into your life. The person Might've not liked who you are, or maybe...They saw something else in you; Which they couldn't swallow and hide.

Don't ask them to be A part of your life, just...Leave it. Even if it hurts. Cause If you actually Think about it, When you're Stable and get into your Happier-mental state, They usually Come back.

Why do they do that?

Cause life is Testing you, Not only you, You are testing yourself.

" If you break someone's Heart and they Still talk to you with the same Excitement and Respect,

Believe me, They really love you. "

- Karma.

When you look into the Person, Nothing might look bad except if you see that They block you from Reaching your goals. If you blocked them once, Reached your goals, Or maybe They Might've just Left you in the middle, And once you see them from a Far distance; Running back...Don't.Do.it.

Life Is Simulation where you should have the knowledge to understand your feelings. To the worst, to the best. Cause the Half of the Year you might be struggling, While the other half, You're happier than ever. Or maybe One year is going to be awesome, The other, not so.

Life is Filled with Surprises, And sometimes, Friends will leave, Relationships which thought might last, Might not. People Make More Friends/Money Than you. But what makes it..Good? All these Feelings are literally Close To Unbearable; Then What's The Huge deal here?

The thing is, At the End, Though Whatever Bad has Come upon you, One thing that might come to your mind is "I will never want to go through that again."

Your Heart might've sank, you've become more "weak", But Know that if you keep on saying this To yourself, This is The Exact Definition of "Self-Sabotage".

CHAPTER FIVE

FEELINGS.

The thing about Feelings Is that, Yes, You experience them; but you can "Give" your Feelings to somebody. Your Happiness Can be Given to someone, And they Decide Whether They can misuse it, or Let that Feeling stay. Your Sorrows Can be Given to Someone, And that "Someone" Has the Opportunity to either keep it that way by leaving, or They keep A bandage around it.

It's The people Who that you give control to your feelings; But in the result, you will be the one to experience the outcome.

HAPPINESS

(though not a negative topic, I'd like to add it)

This is One of the best ones when you'd want to start the Topic About Emotions.

Know that, Happiness is Temporary, but When I mean "Temporary", Happiness Does come back.

Imagine yourself to be Really successful and famous. Of catching your dreams, One thing to keep in mind; You might be Really happy that day and thinking that it's Over, like you Have nothing else to do. But the thing is, To Somewhat Keep it there for A while, Keep Growing, Talk to people, Stay more by building your dreams, Just...Grow!

Remember The people in your life which don't look harmful, Can be the worst than the people who Act/behave like it.

Happiness Isn't also Just Keeping a smile to your face, No. It's about how the mind feels about it.

You should feel free, Safe, Occupied, to be Truly happy.

Happiness isn't also something you can chase, it's some kinda feeling you'll have to let in. Some of us are scared to hold onto and enjoy it, I do have it too sometimes, I

And That Happiness that brings a Smile to your face? You know when you're faking something, But When that Smile Comes from the heart, You are happy at the Exact moment.

This feeling Can be brought down, But you can Always get it back.

So Stay happy and be With people who you Look forward to, Those who don't bring you down.

ANGER

Anger is A Beautiful expression; It could show that you care about something, Demanding for something, letting it out, But in an Aggressive way. Anger isn't A bad thing; Close. But when you shout or scream It out (to someone Especially) You'll keep on shouting until you'll get to a point where you'll think; "Why did I do this?" Anger brings to a mental State where you might end up Happy, Or end up in guilt. (sadness)

Anger isn't something which you scream or shout of, It could be inside you boiling, Whether it's about yourself or somebody else.

Anger Causes Pain, Or relief. But Anger is taken mostly when someone Wants "Revenge"

Revenge Is taken as "Payback", It's hurting Someone or something as an Injury or wrong they suffered; Technically, once again, Paying it back.

Revenge is an intention we take ourselves, to get back at someone for their actions, whether they made you suffer. But the Thing I've seen is that, They used revenge Wrong.

The thing is, They go hurt the person back, Which is a way, Not exactly; though. What I think is when it comes to best revenge, Is to show that you are living better than them. Which jealousy Enters and changes the way they look at you.

SADNESS

The Feeling about being sad is losing how much you loved something which was either taken away, or left you alone.

It's an Emotion where you might end up alone, And realize the truth Behind everything, That's sadness.

When you are alone, you start to realize the truth behind it; It's because you overthink your decisions, and as you come over them, You soon realize how much that person or thing was, and how you were still holding on, later which now, you've let go.

Sadness isn't about tears shedding, it's also how your mind affects it. It makes you worse that you might start to think of ghosting around (Ghosting : Mostly to stop talking to people and go off for a while to fully regain strength from the pain other people caused.) and Come back as A fully-controlled person.

JEALOUSY

Jealousy isn't A healthy Emotion. They feel angry or bitter because they think that another person is trying to take a lover or friend, or a possession, away from them; Or a Possession, a relationship they never had, but want it.

One thing :Don't get jealous, That makes the other person happier. It's best to just not care, And realize you can do better than that. You'll most likely get feelings to top them, But know that as you do these, Know that you are doing this for yourself, And for motivation when you're losing it; Remind yourself about them.

Having a goal? Then work on it. Self-Improvement? Go ahead. Whatever it is, Top them. But don't be hard on yourself... No pain, No gain. But when you realize you're flowing far for the edge to do this, Stop. Slow down, Don't take things too Seriously.

And if you ever Start hearing People talking Bullshit about you, Just understand that you are maturing. After all, They have someone to at least talk about.

"Don't waste your time chasing butterflies. Mend your garden, and the butterflies will come."

Maria Quintana

EMBARRASSED

Embarrassment is something which you've done, Which turned out to be pretty awkward, giving you an uneasy feeling; wishing you'd change things before making them happen.

But, Embarrassment shows in success.

Imagine presenting your goal or doing something relating to your goal. But slowly as you're talking about it, you feel...Embarrassed; That it swallows you whole, Making your mind to stop talking to forget about that dream. The thing is, Never let it slide. If you're Embarrassed about your goal, then Overcome it, especially if you worked really hard at it; nothing should go to waste.

People's words hurt; They really do cut deep. But never put your guard down for them. Why? Cause why ruin your personality to pure enemies. Stand up and face them one by one. Though embarrassing, always make sure to come up in some kind of way.

FEAR

The constant feeling of being anxious, scared about something; Most likely to happen in the future.

One thing about Fear is that It's being misunderstood.

Some people are scared to go outside because of people watching over them, Some people are scared of talking on stage. Some people are afraid to make eye contact. Some people fear failure, being used..This all comes under fear.

But If you are even going to talk it out to someone, (This happens most of the time.) They might just think it's a Phase and you'll get over it. We all Truly need someone who understands us whole, and we should too understand the person's Feelings and opinions better.

One of the best Things to overcome it is Telling yourself that you're not scared of it. As long as you keep on saying it; You'll have some of the Confidence to go actually overcome the fear. The Thing about humans is that, There is nothing which is Impossible when It comes to your goals.

BOREDOM

This isn't exactly a negative feeling , But Being "Bored" Takes you far into Doing stuff which you were never even conscious of.

By what we Naturally take the word "Bored" as, Is when You lose interest at something, or when you currently have nothing to do, so you stay Idle.

But Sometimes Boredom Takes far places.

The thing about being bored is that sometimes, you'd usually turn it up by listening to a podcast, or music, just...doing some

But None of us were born bad, Society had to do something about it.

Next time you see a "Bad person", Realize that they weren't always Like this. There is something which changed in them; whether growing pains, something that they've watched, Their Social Circle...And It would be pretty easy to find out what caused them to do so.

HATE

Hate is something that you have an intense Dislike for.

People Bring up hate in many ways; Gossiping, Giving looks, Teasing, Hurting them mentally, Manipulation and more.

Hate is mostly considered as “Inner Anger” In which many of us have experienced this feeling.

Hatred brings you into a worse mental state; either being hated by so many, or you show hatred to them, But the Real Question is, Why do you care when you are hated by so many? And why Do you waste your energy showing how much you hate someone? Cause One answer comes under this, Karma.

To those who believe or not, Karma can literally do the Job for you. You don’t have to do anything; Cause whatever they do will come back to them. And then they’ll experience pain.

You might be down, hurt right now, But you are going to rise Later while you seem them hurt. And when you do seem them hurt, Don’t go hurt them then too. Do you really want to get hurt again? Exactly.

“ A person able to make you angry, you become a slave of theirs.

A great person is hard on themselves and not anyone.

Even the most Kindest Person has enemies.

If you hate someone, then you are defeated by them.“

DOWNPLAYING

Downplaying is an option, feeling that you are keeping your success rate, Happiness down since you might think that others will not look up to you as competition, and Therefore might like you and be more friendlier, Which will, But you end up with A lot of guilt since you are not able to talk about your success when your with people.

If it does go like this, Don't leave those people, But go and Explore another Social circle that lets you speak freely, Be confident of what you are talking about, And people who would Actually listen to your struggles and success.

We are taught that we should Not go expressing our successes cause People might find it that you are showing off, It is true, But if it someone who

There is One where people will celebrate your success, and there is another one which you do not mind at all; Choose your Circle wisely

CHAPTER SIX

THE THING ABOUT BEING A BEST FRIEND TO SOMEONE.

We've met Many people in our lives; Friends, Strangers, Enemies...But there are people which stop by, And we see common interests, Personalities so similar, Which then is when both people come together and accept each other as "Best friends"

Having A Best friend Is a Different subject when it comes to a Friend.

1 - You shouldn't be the Only one Talking

Best friends Are people you'll rely on. Secrets are more kept towards your best friend, they'll know Mostly everything about you, But if you're the only one speaking, then it's not really a friendship.

Being a best friend to someone is a Two-way street. If they do not talk about their things, just listening to you, They're probably using you. It's Good to be both a Good Listener and a Good talker.

First of all, It's really not fair to be exact, and It can damage both in and out of the friendship. To maintain a friendship; it takes help from the other person to keep it a balance.

2 Value them more than Just a friend.

A best friend is someone who you'll mostly look up to, rather than just a friend. That means You'll listen to them more, Support them, Which they'll also make it feel like home to.

People like "Best friends" are People who are going to stay for a long while; Not knowing when they'll leave...So make them feel like they were meant to be with you.

3 - Common Interests.

Common Interests are important in friendships because they provide a connection for shared experiences and conversations. When the two or more have common interests, conversations usually last longer.

The more you talk about things which both or more find it relatable, They'll mostly make you their comfort person; and Person who understands them better, especially for people who feel like people don't get them.

Common interests do A huge Job in keeping friendships close; for Shared experiences, Conversations and a Sense of belonging.

4 - If they have too many Best friends; Might just be A red flag.

Having too many best friends might stay to be a red flag if the person is unable to maintain close to you.

It could be a red flag if someone has too many best friends because it shows a sign that they are not true to their word or that they are trying to use people. Though if that's their behavior, it's good to know that everyone is different and what is considered a red flag for one person may not be a red flag for another.

Having too many best friends could be a sign of loneliness, and the person may be trying to make a bigger social circle in their life.

5 - - They can love Bombing you.

It could also be a sign that the person is quite manipulative, and is only interested in having friends for what they can get from them. They might also be love bombing you.

It's used to gain control over a person. It starts off with meeting them and giving them attention, affection, and gifts just Like how a normal relationship would go, but later be rude, distant, and cold. They might try to isolate you from your friends and family, Later also to be controlling.

6 - Be there for the thick and thin

When it comes to best friends, nothing should be serious; But sometimes, when Life goes tough for one of them, We should be there for them. These are just some important things you can do in a friendship. It means being there for them when they're down, Going through something, It's Nice to stay for them. And maybe just one day, They will probably stick around for you.

You can listen to them when they need to talk, be there for them in silence. spending time with them, doing things they enjoy, or be a shoulder to cry on.

Let them know that you care about them, it creates bonds stronger.

" If you love someone for their looks, its obsession.

If you love someone for their money, it's interest.

If you love someone because they love you, it's empathy

If you are confused of why you love this person, It is Love. "

CHAPTER SEVEN

Body Language Doesn't Lie.

Communication Has been Universal, But mouths don't always spit the truth.

Everyone Has full-on control over their lives; They are free to say anything they want, They could look innocent while they might be hiding something, They can hate you secretly while they may look interested in you, and they might look okay but they might be truly guilty about something.

Body Language doesn't lie; it's a language of its own. You can understand what a person might be actually telling you by just reading them like a book.

Just say That you're Talking to someone; the next time, Try Looking out for these.

1 - People Raise Their Eyebrows in the sense of discomfort.

They usually Shake their legs, Raise their eyebrows, Have breathing trouble while talking to you. It could mean that you might be scared of you, Or might just have Anxiety. A shaky leg can mean A shaky inner state.

2 - Eyes Speak better.

Eyes can Express mostly everything, Respect, Threat, boredom, non-interested, intimacy...

So the eyes can speak both Negative and positive. When the eyes look dull, not really color in them, then it's quite Negative. Positive? Eyes are either lit up, or widely open, or eyes made up because of a smile.

3 - Spot an Actual smile.

To know if someone is actually smiling, and not purposefully; Is to check the crickles around the eyes to detect whether the smile is actually a real one.

If there are wrinkles around the eyes, it's an actual smile. And if there isn't, then it's a fake one.

4 - Mirroring Body Language.

If they do mirror your actions, Then it just Shows that The conversation is going just fine, And they might be more comfortable around you.

5 - If they look into your eyes for too long, they're lying.

If they tend to stare at you, demanding you to understand that they're saying the truth, They'll most likely look into your eyes for a very long while, which also means their eyes tend to look a lot bigger when they are doing so.

6 - Raised Eyebrows

Raised Eyebrows could show that they are currently listening to you, which also could show a sign of discomfort.

FIRST IMPRESSIONS

When it comes to seeing someone new, we Always put some kind of effort to make ourselves look a bit more superior to them.

The thing About why First Impressions Matter so much is That they're most likely to remember you better than anyone else who made a little bit of an impression or not at all.

To make your First Impressions better, you want it to communicate 3 main things: openness, confidence, and interest.

1 - Eye contact.

Maintain Good eye contact when it comes to this. Breaking eye contact and not looking directly at the person might make them think that you don't like them, and automatically show them to you as poor behavior.

-2 - Smile.

Smile. Smiling makes the other person more comfortable around you, Which they might start to talk more with you. If you smile, They'll most probably smile. And they'll have a Good feeling about you; Also they'll usually come around towards you for help.

3 - Good Speaker = Good listener.

If the person is More of an Introvert-minded, They are most likely not going to talk, so it's best to be a bit more open, talk a lot to maintain it; if you don't want things to turn out awkward. Slowly if you start talking, they'll talk too, If they feel comfortable around you, Of course.

If extroverted, they tend to speak more and say what they feel openly, so it's cool if you speak and go along with them. But don't give them the main head, They can start talking and won't let you speak; Intentionally (or not)

4 - Don't ask too many questions.

Asking too many questions can make them feel nervous. Yes, getting to know them is nice, But it might get them to think negatively, especially when you give that look that you are judging them.

First Impressions are first impressions, And whatever you do can give an effect to your profile of what they've thought of you in their mind.

5 - Speak your opinions; Clearly.

If you are ever going to want to say your feelings more loudly and openly, this should be the time. The person might be someone who walks their way without taking your opinion.

CHAPTER EIGHT

YOUR MIND, WHEN IT COMES TO...

The human mind is quite an awesome possession you're gifted with. Whatever goes on in your head, you're the only one who can view them clearly, And you have the freedom of when you do want to explain what goes on in your head.

The mind is constantly changing and evolving. You are not the same person 10 Years ago. You had different opinions about things and interests you might not have in the present. And How the mind works is truly fascinating. That Everyone has a mind, But thinks Differently; But they're are some things which we all stand for in common.

THE MIND WHEN IT COMES TO BELIEFS

We All have different ways of thinking, And that also comes to beliefs.

Some people Pray everyday, some people in a week, month, or never really did. Most people have their own different cultures in which they were raised that way to believe as such, Or people have changed their way of thinking to another belief.

A news Back long ago there was a case where people all over the country were praying for a child with something called an "incurable ailment" (an illness that explains that someone with it can die in days, weeks, months or more than a year.) was trapped in a flooded mine with a few miners as well. What news was to come later was They were rescued. Therefore people started talking about how The prayer was effective and how the miners talked about them praying during the rescue.

Prayer is a realization of your heart's desire. While you pray, you are going to mentally have a picture of them, or just a thought in your head, and people believe that they get their answer solely because of trust between you and them, and acceptance.

From this case, Prayer and beliefs have become a part of each other's lives. There is another belief that you shouldn't ask the person/thing you're praying to for things which you can do to earn them, then they wouldn't allow your request. It's now a belief that Most people believe in, Why? It's said that it's just something where you'll have to work hard to earn them. According to me, (whether you believe or not) I think it gives out a great message that if you want something then do what's right for it.

Another thing great for belief is great that whatever you believe, sometimes, gives motivation for you to do better. Just like the one above, you are meant to work hard for things in which you will be rewarded for. Some things don't just work if you keep on praying.

THE MIND WHEN IT COMES TO PEOPLE

People are a part of our lives. You were meant to see one coming and leave, Without any warning.

One person Can give this great impression, and can leave at any point. What's the thing here? Don't Expect anyone to stay. Your best friend will not be there one day, That one popular person will not stay like that forever. The person you like might not like you back. You are going to definitely Experience something sad at some point...The only thing to do is deal with it.

The thing is People's Thoughts are forgotten, dead, abandoned At some point, But you made them feel will not be the case; You will never forget how you or they felt in that memory or time.

We all had enemies or some good friends who'd been with us, Might've left, might've stayed. But notice how you separate the good and bad between people? Why? Because you tend to understand, cover and know each other better with the people who you consider as people you should be around with, because of that positive energy. And for the other side for people who mislead you, and don't seem to get you.

They are people who can take you far, or keep you grounded. You will definitely come to a point of asking a friend or someone for advice and helping them reach that goal. People have different thinking and opinions about eac

Just like how you've set different roles for each person you see, Imagine, How many people would've thought of you the same way? There are many versions of you in each person's mind.

Some people see you as fun, Loyal, kind; others rude, cold-hearted...Why?

Sometimes, we ourselves are quick to judge. "Never judge a Book by its cover" Is A quote, as much as many people follow it; But there are just these times where we accidently do it, It's how we humans get some things wrong. It's what makes us, us.

And gossip, People recommendations are also what Makes people think differently about you. Let's say you've never stepped outside before. You'd ask other people for advice whether you'd want to step outside, some people will say yes,as they say it's necessary...Some people will say no, Saying the world is a bad place. Same thing goes for when they talk about you. People will have different opinions and tell you and might (honestly) explain How they view you. Trying to change one person's mind? you are and will be bad in someone's life, And you cannot change that one person's mind.

15 Second Personality Test.

Let's try something real quick - Think about an animal.

If you were going to become an animal at some point, which one would you be?

The animal you also thought does not exist, think about another one.

If both of these animals did not exist, Which other animal would you be?

Keep these three animals in mind, and in order.

Animal = Personality

1 - The animal You first thought of is how you want to be seen By people.

2 - The second animal you've thought of is How you are actually seen by people.

3 - The third animal is How you actually are, instead of people's opinions about

THE MIND WHEN IT COMES TO FEARS.

When you have the mindset of becoming someone bigger, You will worry, you will fear.

"What Will Society Think?

Will I regret this?

Am I sure that I will make it?

It's too far away, Should I Be doing this?"

It's where you do know what you want, But it's fear that takes it away. Fear takes dreams away. It lures you so far close to it that You'd somewhat feel embarrassed to make that goal happen. Maybe you start to find it quite cringe, or

You start taking people's opinions.

One thing about success is that some rules are meant to be broken. Maybe you won't meet your parents' expectations if you do want to reach that goal, Maybe you will have to sacrifice someone or something for it,or just maybe, you have to push down those fears and embarrassment, just so you could reach there.

Fear and the mind are quite connected, and when this "Fear " takes over you, you will probably think of scenarios that won't exactly happen...But when this happens, You should think about focusing on the present, Whatever is going to happen, will happen. People will be watching, and will forget about it at any point in their life. Maybe if you weren't able to catch that goal just yet, It just signs that you are just close enough to raise a hand high once more or again to reach it, Life could be testing you, after all.

Another thing is, If you do have anxiety or fear, Just know that you'll have to go through it if you do want to rise, You actually need that anxiety. When we stay quiet, Slowly just watch and not do anything, you realize the truth behind it. But when I say that when you do have that anxiety, you should have it knowing you will get over it. You'll look at the world around you,and realize nobody is stopping for anyone or anything. You'll have to find a spot and make sure you'll rise, and then come back prepared to face the other side of life.

People say that "The Depressed makes the best songs." With that, The person who fears and has anxiety, Will be seen as the greatest once overcoming it, Overcoming fears makes you unrecognizable.

`` The word F-E-A-R Has two meanings :

Face Everything And Rise.

Forget Everything And Run.

The choice is yours. ``

- Zig Ziglar

THE MIND WHEN IT COMES TO THE OLD, LIFE/ DEATH

There will Be a day, someday, where you'll come to a point that your life will end, and we'll never know which date it will be. People will remember you, But at one point to another, they will forget you; It's the truth.

That's why People say that to live life to the fullest, with the opportunity you have now, try to maintain and have fun. Life comes with regrets and fears, Joy and fun, Loneliness and anxiety. What's the best part? If you were able to experience every feeling.

The thing about both life and death is, nothing is fair. Lives are different; Whether they have something you don't, or you have something they don't. If you do want to change your life around, Some things will change, some things can't.

Comparison is the thief of all Joy. When you compare lives, Things, stuff, which other people have which might have and not be just as good as yours, Know that it isn't necessary to have that thing, life or anything necessarily. Your main mission is to know how to keep yourself happy from everything which doesn't make you happy. Happy keeps you long enough, so keep it that way.

One thing I learned about staying alive for pretty long enough is Actually, Staying active and happy.

Even if you are middle aged, you will come and learn to a point that you are growing old, and things are going to change. What most Old people do Is stay at home and waste their lives on tv, or watch things move and grow while you slowly fade. What's the actual thing to do is You should be active if you want to live longer.

Being old Means that you are going to have to enjoy things just like how they say to enjoy childhood, And by staying way more happier, It's the time where you'll have to stop focusing on the bad and stay alive and breathe in the moment you are present with. Rather than staying at home and reviewing, playing old memories of the past and grieve that you're growing old and forgotten, You should go outside, learn new things, Stay updated, Go around with your friends.

The thing that actually got me thinking about this is my grandfather.

Some other grandparents tend to die a bit early, and What I've seen in most of their lifestyle was they ended up staying at home, watched television and Laughed and smiled a bit less (Maybe family issues) And from My grandfather, He stayed positive, Stayed loved and meet his close people, spend time outdoors and most importantly Laughed, like, a lot.

It's said that Laughing adds more time to your clock (up to fifteen years most probably) and It's also about staying peaceful and happy when you are growing old. If you wanna see the world for a bit more, stay happier.

It can be tough staying in a world like this and finding happiness is mostly impossible, But finding it is worth it.

Another thing is, Seeking advice from the old is that they will probably give you a better look into life or let you see the way they see life.

I still Remember me asking a grandma, we were talking, got to a point where I asked her whether there is something she regrets and wishes she went back in time and changed.

She thought and thought, and came up with something :

" I Regret how I never risked things, Or else I would've been far off. "

She continued; " I was never grateful for anything, But now, Old and tired, I wish I was at least...Grateful. "

The fact I realized that whatever she said, Is whatever I or what some people thought about themselves, She wasn't surprised, And went on talking about its normal to think it that way. Well I went on, asking how she talked about regretting not risking a few things.

" I Thought not risking was a good idea, so I never took that path, I thought speaking on stage, starting a business with no experience... Was a risk and I'd be Better off if I didn't. "

She went on saying a few more, Explained in my way :

In Web-series and movies, And in a few people's lives, It shows that during their teenage life, Something...Just happens, Something in which that Changes their lives and becomes an impact in their life.. They just wait for it, Pray for something and there are obstacles and then, there. Their goal or something happens, with some or no effort.

She said that someone else told her this, and that person waited and prayed for that miracle, or just...appeared.

At some point, they realized nothing is going to happen by just staying silent, So they rose and tried actually reaching that goal.

There are things we regret at some point, whether you'd try making your life perfect...Just something, always, regret.

CHAPTER NINE

DREAMS MAY FADE, MAY NOT.

Sometimes, The dream relationship, job, goal you had could slowly turn into a feeling or thing you had before. The thing about saying you are going to achieve that dream is to plan and think of whether you are actually going to do it or not.

Things we thought as kids are going to stay as memories, Or whether you'd actually want to achieve them. But going back to the first paragraph, if you were letting go of that dream while you were in the middle of achieving it, you'd start to push yourself to fight for that feeling when you started thinking of this goal you had, or you would give it away.

At this point, you have to know what you want.

Everyone regrets something, so, It kinda doesn't matter. You were meant to regret something in your life, By choosing something you thought you would have a change in you, or any other examples you could think of.

Before you get into something, Like making a decision or some friendship you just got in, Do I need this? Am I right for this? Will I make it? Is that you want it just because your friends are going for it too? Or you just found the title interesting? Or are you desperate?

And then you'd slowly lose it, and then you'd disappoint people who thought you might make the idea happen, or your past self.

There are many things I regret doing, so here is A somewhat list incase for your next plan have a more chance of working :

Plan it out.

The thing about making something happen is that Plan it out, and tell a few people about your idea, as soon as it works, people would totally be around to see you rise.

To be honest, In making this book, One thing I didn't do was plan this out. I got so excited about the idea and the fact that I didn't think it out, so possibly, I ran out of ideas, But then I had something to back it up. The book would have been sold a while ago if I just did but, I took more time.

Absorb knowledge

If you are going to do a goal you've been doing for a while, It's most likely you have already taken inspiration for someone or something to do it. (If you haven't then do it)

If you are going to write a book, Read other books and understand how they do it.

If you want to start a business, Go to someone who'd explain a few tips about it or take courses.

If you want to be a singer, Learn how they write songs, or practice on your voice.

Keep your goal hidden until you make it.

The thing about sharing your goal with so many people is that if you are not going to be making it the first time, You'll slowly let go of it since you would be afraid of whether people would judge you.

It's how most of us stop making it to the top, Why would they think? What would they say? It's best to stay silent until you reach it.

Be careful with what you say

Words are sometimes like small needles on your skin, the more it is, the more it's seen on you and the more you'd cover it bleeding. Bleeding shows how you are feeling internally by those words, but in public, you'd put bandages so no one would see them. Words do have a lot of meaning and feeling into them.

Those needles will be in your skin until you decide to pull them out and change yourself about those negative comments about people.

I'm not saying those needles might all be bad but, Words like be kind too, so pull those needles which don't deserve to be in your mind and affect you.

Epilouge

" Two Faced, A Villain, A Hero" Explains a basic introduction to which no person thinks the same, Infact, we do come together, somewhat, equally, Teaching you simple tricks to get along and stay put where you are right now.

Few things to keep in mind -

We are meant to be bad.

There are different versions of you alive in people's minds.

Sadly, Most of the time, Our feelings don't matter.

People leave you when you are addicted to them.

To be the happiest among the sadness.

Focus on things you can control than can't.

Do things that actually make you happy.

Smiling isn't just about making/showing the face that you are happy.

Having that mindset that "They" are the "Only one for you" is the worst mindset.

Maybe people do come back cause they couldn't find someone to replace you with.

Stop suffering Imaginatively.

People know what exactly they are doing.

Don't beg anyone to stay.

Some traumas never heal, that's scars.

Focus on being better, not perfect.

" You Shouldn't climb the mountains for the world to see you,

- But for you to see the world. "

- David McCullough Jr.

www.ingramcontent.com/pod-product-compliance
Lightning Source LLC
LaVergne TN
LVHW070258170826
845679LV00030B/1413

9798891331228